SACRAMENTO
KINGS

Kings
43

SACRAMENTO
KINGS

TOM PETERSON

CREATIVE EDUCATION

Photo Credit: Creative Education would like to thank NBA photographer Ron Koch (New York City) for the color photography in this series.

Published by Creative Education Inc., 123 South Broad Street, Mankato, Minnesota 56001.

ISBN: 0-88682-207-6

It seemed as if the early settlers of Sacramento, California, could do no wrong. Sacramento started out back in 1840 as little more than a tiny fort and a few log cabins, but time would soon change the settlers' fortunes.

From the discovery of gold at Sutter's mill in 1848, to the naming of Sacramento as the state capital in 1854, the city of Sacramento would play an important role in the development of California.

"Our city's good fortune continues," proclaimed well-known Sacramento businessman Joe Benvenuti in early April of 1985. "It is my pleasure to announce that the NBA has granted our formal request for a professional basketball franchise. From now on, the sixth team in the NBA's Central Division will be known as the Sacramento Kings."

As far as their fans were concerned, the new Sacramento Kings could do no wrong during their very first season, 1985-86, in the California capital city. They won only 37 games that year, but to the sell-out crowds that packed Sacramento's Arco Arena for each game, that was just fine. The fans were just happy to have a professional team to support.

Los Angeles sportswriter Pat Murphy attended one of those early games and came away with the feeling that Sacramento just might boast the most enthusiastic crowd in the league.

Kings

They're certainly among the loudest," wrote Murphy. "But I couldn't help wondering whether or not the Sacramento fans were cheering with the realization that they were watching a team with regal roots. The Kings, after all, are direct descendants of the old Rochester and Cincinnati Royals. I'd like to think that the Sacramento fans are aware that they've inherited a tradition shaped by legendary NBA figures such as Bob Wanzer, Alex Hannum, Maurice Stokes, Jack Twyman, Oscar Robertson, Jerry Lucas, Nate Archibald and many others."

The great grandfathers of today's Sacramento Kings were the Rochester Royals who got their start at the close of World War II in the old National Basketball League. In their first season, 1945-46, the Royals surprised the two time defending champion Fort Wayne Pistons of Indiana in the semifinals and then swept the championship series from the Sheboygan Redskins of Wisconsin.

The Royals franchise helped capture the imagination of the American sports fan because of the multi-talented players who comprised their roster. Their 1946 championship team included future New York Knick coach Red Holzman, future pro football star Otto Graham, Del Rice, who would later become a St. Louis Cardinal catcher, and Chuck Connors, who would become famous as a television and movie actor.

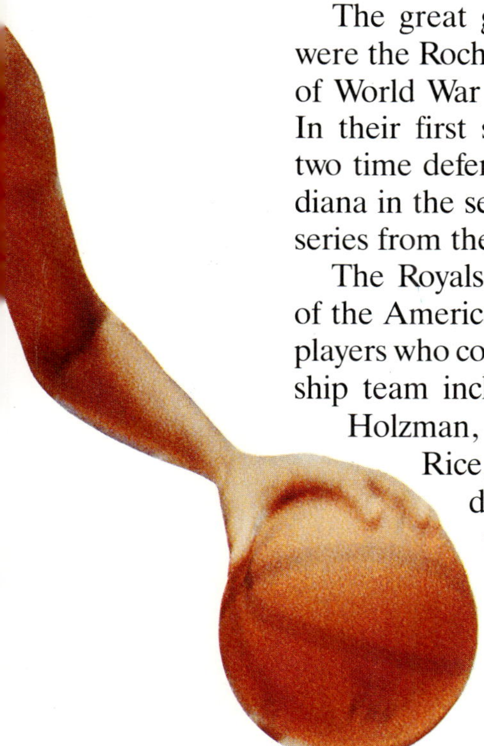

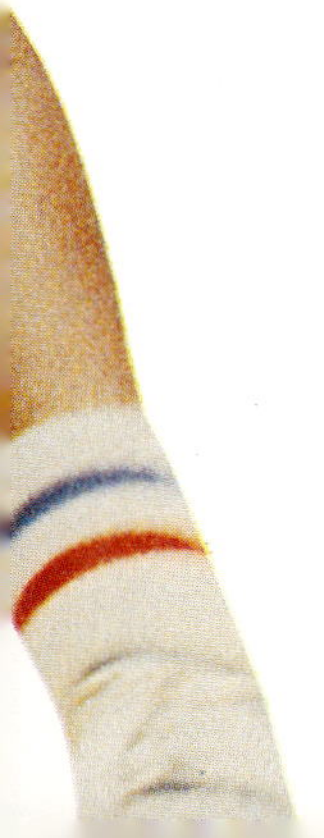

Swingman Harold Pressley was selected in the first round of the 1986 draft by the Kings.

In 1948-49, the Royals and the Minneapolis Lakers jumped to a rival league called the Basketball Association of America. The Lakers had 6-foot-10 George Mikan, the most dominant young player of the decade, but the scrappy Royals still managed to finish first in the division that year.

The following season, the NBL and the BAA merged to become the league we know today as the National Basketball Association. Within two seasons the Royals would once again fight their way to the top. Arnie Risen, Bob Davies, Bob Wanzer, Red Holzman, Arnie Johnson and Jack Coleman were the core players of the early NBA team. They were a close-knit group of guys who supported each other through good times and bad. The result of their teamwork was a world title.

"Royals Top Knicks in Final Minute For Crown," read the April 21, 1951 headline in the *New York Times*. History shows that this particular championship series finally elevated pro basketball into the national limelight. Not only was it a dramatic and spectacular series, but it involved two teams from New York, the communications capital of the sports world.

Although the Royals would not quite maintain the quality and excitement of their championship season, they did continue to make the playoffs over the next couple of years. And the club took a definite turn for the better when the 1955 draft yielded forward Jack Twyman and center Maurice Stokes. Both were gifted players who soon became inseparable friends.

Maurice Stokes (12) battles with John Kerr of the Syracuse Nats at Madison Square Garden.

Nats
10
ROYALS
15

Overnight, Twyman became one of the top scorers in the league. Meanwhile, his friend Stokes was dominating the boards. The broad shouldered, 6-foot-7 Cincinnati center became the top rebounder in the entire NBA on his way to earning 1956 Rookie of the Year honors.

Stokes and Twyman spent three action packed seasons together until tragedy struck in 1958. Stokes had just completed another fine season when he learned that he had been stricken with encephalitis. The crippling brain disease ended his career. The once graceful basketball star was left paralyzed and hospitalized.

It was a shocking blow to Twyman who took it upon himself to help his friend to the very end. Twyman became Stokes' legal guardian and raised funds for his rehabilitation. Each year Twyman assembled pro basketball stars in Monticello, New York, to play a benefit game for the Maurice Stokes fund.

About the same time as the Stokes' tragedy the Rochester Royals were beginning to come up losers, both on and off the court. Their declining record translated into smaller crowds. Smaller crowds meant less money to purchase good players. And without good players, their record would only get worse.

In 1957-58 the Royals packed up their gear and moved from upstate New York to the Rhineland country of Cincinnati, Ohio. There

Jack Twyman

They hoped Oscar would pack the Cincinnati Garden.

they hoped to change their luck by staking claim to the nation's most exciting college player, the University of Cincinnati's Oscar Robertson.

"They hoped Oscar would pack the Cincinnati Garden," wrote Zander Hollander in the *Official Encyclopedia of Pro Basketball.* "And while that dream was never fully realized, Robertson did have a significant impact on the fortunes of the team. The Royals still finished last in the Western Conference, but they won 14 more games in Oscar's rookie season of 1960-61 than they had the year before, and by the following season they were solid contenders for the league title."

Oscar Robertson

16
ROYALS

Born on November 24, 1938 in Charlotte, Tennessee, Oscar was still a youngster when he moved north to the basketball country of Indianapolis, Indiana. His talents as a basketball player were evident even then. Single-handedly he took Crispus Attucks High School to 45 straight victories and two consecutive state titles. As a collegian with the Cincinnati Bearcats, Oscar led the nation in scoring for three straight years and captured All-American honors.

"Don't try to describe the man," said Jack Twyman after Robertson had set the league on fire in his first NBA season, averaging an astounding 30 points a game as a rookie. "You can watch him, you can enjoy him, you can appreciate him, but you can't adequately describe him. Whatever is needed at the time comes out because Oscar has complete physical control of his body. It's not any one thing, it's his completeness that amazes you."

Soon it seemed that every player in the NBA had a

You can watch him, you can enjoy him, you can appreciate him, but you can't adequately describe him.

classic "Big O" story to tell. "I remember we were playing the Royals one night," said Boston Celtic Tom Meschery, "and somehow I ended up guarding Oscar after a switch. Well, Oscar throws the ball behind his back, heads for the basket and leaves me behind. It was a fantastic move, split second like always with him. But just as the ball goes in, the referee calls traveling. Oscar got real excited and starts screaming at him, 'How can you call that traveling? You never saw that move before.' "

Jerry Lucas was a go-get-em player who would fight for loose balls and battle ferociously for rebounds.

In 1963-64 Oscar and the Royals were joined by Jerry Lucas, the three time All-American from Ohio State. At 6-foot-8, Lucas lacked Robertson's finesse, but he had talents and qualities all his own. Jerry was a hustling player who would fight for loose balls and battle ferociously under the boards. Whether he was snatching a rebound, setting a pick for Robertson, or moving into position for his own set shot, Lucas was one tough competitor.

In each of Lucas' first three years, the Cincinnati Royals advanced to the playoffs. One of their most memorable squads took the floor during the 1965-66 season. In addition to Robertson and Lucas, Cincinnati featured three true crowd pleasers in Adrian Smith, Wayne Embry and Happy Hairston.

The ringleader of this colorful crew was Jack McMahon, an intense coach who had starred for the 1958 NBA champion St. Louis Hawks. McMahon would work himself into a frenzy on the sidelines, and a loss would upset him long after the final buzzer had sounded.

"I don't want to talk about it," McMahon would still be saying a day or two after a game. "If that referee had called . . . I don't want to talk about it." Silence. "Did you see them hit Lucas on the tip? I don't want to talk about it."

Amid all the craziness, the Royals did manage to earn several playoff confrontations with the archrival Boston Celtics during the mid-sixties, but Cincinnati always came out on the short end.

The "Big O" in action: Oscar Robertson (14), regarded by many as the finest all-around basketball player ever, battles Bill Russell.

ROYALS
14
BOSTON
25

In an attempt to capture some of the Celtic magic for themselves, the Royals hired former Boston guard Bob Cousy to coach the team in 1969. Cousy brought along the same fast break offense that had made him famous, but it was one that didn't suit Lucas and Robertson. As a result, Cousy soon announced that he would trade away the two aging legends.

Though the Cincinnati fans were saddened by Cousy's decision, it was a beneficial move for all concerned. Over the years Lucas' knees had taken a beating, and he had become too slow for Cousy's up-tempo style of basketball. As for Robertson, he continued to excel after leaving Cincinnati, eventually leading Lew Alcindor and the Milwaukee Bucks to the 1970-71 NBA title.

The departure of Robertson and Lucas opened the way for a young rookie by the name of Nate Archibald. Better known as "Tiny," Archibald joined the Royals in 1970 as a second round draft choice from the University of Texas at El Paso. With Oscar Robertson gone, coach Cousy had instructed assistant coach Draff Young to

"find me a guard who can penetrate and run the show." Young took a chance and chose Archibald.

At 5-foot-11, 150 pounds, Nate was the smallest man in the NBA and many were skeptical of his ability. "I'm used to that kind of stuff," sighed Archibald, who grew up in New York City's rugged South Bronx area. "As a kid I wanted to play basketball all the time. I'd find out there was going to be a game and I'd be there waiting. The older guys would always say, 'Well, we'll let him play, he's small, he'll get tired and quit.' But I never would."

After Archibald's first season the Royals changed homes again, this time becoming the Kansas City-Omaha Kings. Thanks to Tiny, the fans in those two cities were in for a rare treat. It was the season in which he became the first man in NBA history to lead the league in both scoring, 34 points per game, and assists, 11.4 per game.

"Left out of the cold statistics," wrote basketball historian Bob Ryan, "are the number of times the dynamic little man weaved his way through gigantic forests of limbs to flip in an acrobatic basket; or how he would lead a fast break and suddenly make a 35-foot bounce pass to a cutting teammate who no one else saw for an easy two points." So dominant was Archibald that Cousy all but turned over the entire team to him, making the little guard the center of the offense.

The older guys would always say, "Well, we'll let him play, he's small, he'll get tired and quit." But I never would.

That was okay with Archibald's teammates. With Tiny drawing all the attention on the court, Matt Guokas, Tom Van Arsdale, Nate Williams and Sam Lacey all found themselves in the clear that year, prompting Guokas to say, "Tiny makes us all look big."

Despite Tiny's heroics, the Kings didn't quite make the playoffs in 1973-74. It was the same story in 1974-75, a year in which the team was distracted by a mid-season coaching change. Cousy was fired and Phil Johnson was named to replace him.

Again in 1975-76, the team moved to a new home base, this time just down the road to Kansas City, Missouri. For the Kings, the highlight of that otherwise undistinguished season came with the announcement of the NBA's All-Star team. Kareem Abdul-Jabbar was the center, flanked by George McGinnis and Rick Barry at the forwards. The backcourt players were "Pistol Pete" Maravich and the Kansas City Kings' very own Nate Archibald.

That tribute to Tiny made Coach Johnson's next move appear outrageous. Just prior to the 1976-77 season, Johnson helped trigger a decision by Kings management to trade Archibald to the New Jersey Nets for two future draft choices. There were cries of outrage from the Kansas City fans. These cries were quieted, however, when the draft choices resulted in the selection of Otis Birdsong in 1977 and Phil Ford in 1978.

At 5-foot-11, 150 pounds, Nate "Tiny" Archibald proved that little guys with ability can star in the NBA.

NEW YORK
15
Kings
10

Phil Ford

Birdsong, the smooth shooting 6-foot-4 guard from the University of Houston, swiftly unseated forward Scott Wedman to become the Kings' new scoring leader. Ford, the 1978 college basketball player of the year, joined Birdsong in the backcourt as the quarterback of the team.

Ford and Birdsong brought a bright new spirit to the team. "They're like two peas in a pod," said new head coach Lowell "Cotton" Fitzsimmons who took over for Johnson in 1978-79. "They're a couple of professional comedians who just happen to play ball in the NBA. They're the guys who keep this team loose, and you gotta be loose to play basketball."

But Fitzsimmons' Kings knew when to laugh and when to work. With Ford, Birdsong, Wedman, Lacey and Bill Robinzine leading the way, the club blazed to a 48-34 record in 1978-79,

But Fitzsimmons' Kings knew when to laugh and when to work.

earning their first division title in 27 years. Although Kansas City was eliminated in the fifth and deciding game of the playoffs by the Phoenix Suns, the team, for the first time since the 1960s, had triggered high expectation for the future.

The high hopes were dashed the next year when the Milwaukee Bucks won the Midwest Division by two games over the Kings. While Kansas City seemed to have the nucleus to compete with the NBA elite, the team never seemed to reach their potential.

Injuries to Ford, Wedman, Lacey and several others during the 1980-81 season forced coach Fitzsimmons to rely on nearly two dozen different starting lineups during the season. Although the Kings managed to make it to the playoffs, people questioned their desire to win.

When asked to predict Kansas City's chances in the opening playoff series against Portland, however, Fitzsimmons defended his players. "In terms of individual talent, I think you would have to say there is not a lot here. But there are a lot of teams that have losing records that could be just as good as we are if

Otis Birdsong

they had our chemistry. Nobody's going to beat us badly in the playoffs. We've got too much character."

Sure enough, the Kings went on to defeat the Trail Blazers in the mini-series. Next, in the conference semi-finals they defeated the Phoenix Suns in seven games. Though the Kings were finally eliminated in the conference finals by Houston, they went home with their heads held high. After all, their seven victories in 15 playoff games were the most in franchise history.

But this was not enough to satisfy a championship hungry front office. On June 9, 1981, the Kings traded All-Stars Otis Birdsong and Scott Wedman, a move that drastically altered the chemistry of the team. The trading would continue when on November 10, 12-year veteran Sam Lacey was swapped to New Jersey for 6-foot-5 forward Mike Woodson and a first round draft pick. The personnel changes threw the club into a terrible tailspin. The Kings finished 1981-82 with a record of 30-52, a ten win drop over the previous season.

Though the Kings were finally eliminated in the conference finals by Houston, they went home with their heads held high.

Twelve-year veteran Sam Lacey was traded to the New Jersey Nets in 1981 for Mike Woodson and a first round draft pick.

WALK
41
44

MAHORN
14
Kings
25
bulle
14
WASHINGTON

The next three years, 1982-84, would continue to bring disappointment to the Kings and their fans. Numerous losses and low attendance would cast a long shadow over the franchise. Although players such as Mike Woodson and Reggie Theus would occasionally bring a victory for coach Fitzsimmons, the Kings remained near the bottom of the standings.

The Kings would play one more season in Kansas City, 1984-85, before moving to their current home in Sacramento. The final year in Kansas City began on a dismal note with the Kings losing eight of their first nine homestands. Coach Jack McKinney, who had replaced Cotton Fitzsimmons, resigned and Phil Johnson, who had coached the Kings in the mid-1970s, took over once again.

Johnson did manage to make the team competitive before the season expired. But it was not enough. After 13 years in Kansas City, the club was now looking else-

. . . Kansas City began on a dismal note with the Kings losing eight of their first nine homestands.

where for its future.

The news hit on April 3, 1985, when the NBA announced that the special committee appointed to look into the Kings' relocation to Sacramento, California had recommended approval of the move. No one in California cheered louder than the six Sacramento businessmen who had purchased the team back in June, 1983 for $10.5 million.

Ray Williams (25), a promising young guard out of the University of Minnesota, was tabbed by the Kings to replace Otis Birdsong in the early 80s.

"Sacramento is a growing, thriving world-class city," beamed part owner Joe Benvenuti. "We're confident that the entire community will welcome the Kings with open arms and support our ultimate goal, to bring a championship to Sacramento."

Five days after the season ended, the franchise was officially moved to Sacramento. There, the Kings players found the royal welcome mat spread out before them. Benvenuti had been right. Sacramento was a city bursting at the seams to show its support for professional basketball.

"The Kings had much to celebrate their first year," wrote an analyst in the *Official NBA Guide*. "The move from Kansas City paid off in the stands as the Kings sold all 10,333 tickets for every game in their temporary arena. After a two year absence, they also made the playoffs, thanks to the steady play of Reggie Theus, who averaged 18.3 points and was third in the league in assists. LaSalle Thompson tied for eighth in the league with 9.6 rebounds per game and Eddie Johnson, who became the sixth man when Terry Tyler moved into the starting lineup, led the Kings with an 18.7 scoring average."

Versatile Reggie Theus was acquired in a trade with Chicago in 1984. In 1986-87 he led the club in six different statistical categories.

It was this support that highlighted the Kings first year in Sacramento. Win or lose, the fans of Sacramento would turn out to encourage their club. But the Sacramento fans were not content with simply celebrating the usual milestones of a NBA season. Sparked by unbounded first year enthusiasm, they seemed to applaud every move, play or point. A deafening roar shook the stands when Reggie Theus scored the first basket in Arco Arena, and when LaSalle Thompson hit the first free throw and grabbed the first rebound, and when Otis Thorpe made the first assist. And so it went.

On April 22, 1986, the Kings played host to the Denver Rockets before the 42nd sold-out game of the season at Arco Arena. Down 0-2 in the best of five opening series of the playoffs, the Kings went into the game knowing that the club had won all eleven Tuesday night games in the past year. But this night the streak ended. Denver downed the Kings, 113-98, to end Sacramento's inaugural season.

In 1984-85 and 1985-86, LaSalle Thompson was among the NBA's top rebounders.

Kings
Kings
NETS

The move to Sacramento had been a success on and off the court. The Kings had the fan support which had been lacking in Kansas City and a young team whose best games appeared to be ahead of them.

But the future was farther ahead than most King fans assumed. The emotion and energy that had carried the Kings through their first season in Sacramento quickly disappeared. By February of the 1987 season, the Kings were a disappointing 13-42 and seeking some direction. In an attempt to rejuvenate the team, coach Phil Johnson was fired and replaced by interim coach Jerry Reynolds.

But as in most instances, this provided little help and the Kings failed to reach the playoffs. If the Kings were to improve in the future, the personnel would have to improve.

To help guide the Kings personnel decisions in the future, Sacramento signed NBA Hall-of-Famer Bill Russell to a seven year contract in April 1987. Russell would become the head coach beginning with the 1987-88 season

If the Kings were to improve in the future, the personnel would have to improve.

and within four years he would have the option of becoming general manager and eventually president.

The players Russell led into the 1988 season included Joe Kleine, Ed Pinckney, Reggie Theus, Derek Smith and rookie Kenny Smith. It was the rookie, Smith, on whom Russell was placing much of his team's hopes.

As a guard at the University of North Carolina, Smith led his team to a 115-22 record and finished his career as

Kenny Smith was tabbed by coach Bill Russell to lead the Kings back to the playoffs.

North Carolina's all-time leader in assists. It was hoped that Smith's leadership would guide the Kings back to the playoffs.

But even the best laid plans of Bill Russell could not help the Kings. Plagued by injuries and general poor play, Sacramento failed to live up to the high expectations set by Russell and his staff. By the middle of the season the team and the coaching staff seemed to be in disarray.

In particular, strained relationships between the staff and players seemed to be a problem. As a result, Russell's assistant Willis Reed would leave the team, and eventually even Russell himself would call it quits. Into his place would once again step Jerry Reynolds, who had coached the Kings prior to Russell. But even his efforts would prove unsuccessful and for the second straight season the Kings failed to make the playoffs.

The 1987-88 season had been a dismal return to the past for the Kings. A poor record and sagging attendance created problems the Kings franchise knew too well. If Sacramento is to redirect their path in the 1990s it will take patience. A characteristic that brought good fortune to the early settlers of Sacramento; and one that will serve the Kings and their fans just as well.